9 TIPS

to Up
Your

CREATIVE
GENIUS

Patti Dobrowolski

Copyright © 2018, Patti Dobrowolski, v.1.0
ISBN: 978-0-9839856-3-1

Interior design: J.L Saloff
Cover design: Scott Ward
Editing: Patricia Kyritsi Howell
Typography: Light up the World
All illustrations, Patti Dobrowolski

Print edition, 2018

For the Creative
Genius Inside You

FORESIGHT

If you were to gather a room full of amazing people and ask, "Which of you consider yourself to be a creative genius?" It's likely that fewer than 10% will raise their hands.

I think it's time we each reclaim and empower our own creative genius and give it the recognition it deserves.

This book is designed to jumpstart your ability to access your unique creative visions and activate them in your life.

Big love, Patti ♡

CREATIVE GENIUS
TIP #1

Inner critics take up way too much head space, keeping you from getting in touch with your creative genius. And it will keep you from living your dreams.

Your inner critic doesn't want you to take risks, it wants you to play it safe, stick to what you know, sleepwalking through your life. While your creative

genius wants to wake you up and get you engaged in all that is possible in your life.

When you start to say something negative to yourself, remember, that those inner words pack just as much punch as any you might actually speak out loud.

It's a wild world we are living in. You need to be proactive and create some reminders about how great you are, something you have on hand when those negative voices try to run the show.

TIP #1:

Right now, get some paper and write a few words or a saying, anything you find inspiring and carry it around with you.

Something like..."I am smart, capable, open, loving" or draw a picture of some of the attributes that you want to embody and carry it with you or put it somewhere you can see it every day! Whenever you start down that negative path, read what you have written and believe it.

CREATIVE GENIUS TIP #2

PRACTICE GRATITUDE

Gratitude is the ultimate wheel greaser. It reminds you that each moment is precious, meaningful, and important.

Yep, I know some things are hard to be grateful for, but when you shift your perspective from that of a victim who wonders, "Why is this terrible thing happening to me?!" to a place where you are curious, asking "What is this situation or person trying to teach me?" then everything changes.

Whether you and I like all the things that happen to us is a different conversation, but know that whatever is happening in your world, it is there to help you see something about yourself and hopefully nourish the creative genius you.

If at first you can't figure out why something is happening, put on your detective outfit, grab a magnifying glass and look for clues until you figure out the reason.

While you are looking for clues, it's just as important to step back to see your world from a higher perspective.

Ask yourself these questions:

Does this feel familiar?
Is it a pattern?
If so, when did ??
I experience this
before?

TIP #2:
Grab a piece of paper and try to draw the pattern as if you are drawing a treasure map for yourself. Where is the buried treasure in this experience? What tools do you have that will help you to dig it up?

Then, go about your day, looking for more clues. Each time you get some insight, send a big ball of love out there into the universe for helping you solve the mystery!

17

CREATIVE GENIUS
TIP #3

TRY SOMETHING NEW

The creative genius part of your brain is like a pattern making machine. It needs you to show it new patterns to encourage it and keep it flexible.

It's so easy to do the same thing over and over again every day. You get up, make your morning cup of coffee, get your children off to school, and head off to work. At the end of the day, you come home, eat dinner, watch the same shows on the telly and then trundle to bed about the same time.

Maybe you feel you can control what your response will be to almost anything that happens in your day by following your well-worn routine.

To try something new, you must ask the universe to help you up your creative genius. Then get ready, because you are about to change and grow into someone new, which means you have to let go of the past and business as usual.

To become someone new, you have to crack open some space in your routine to allow the magic to occur. Magic things are happening all the time. You don't really need to be Harry Potter with a wand. The big secret is your attitude is your wand, so go make some magic!

TIP #3:

Each day, no matter how many demands come your way that you don't seem to have control over, try to find any small opening where you can do things differently. It can be buying a different kind of tea, walking your dog on a different street, sitting in a different chair in your living room. The important thing is that you are signaling to the universe that you are ready to make new patterns. Be open to new ways of moving through your day so you are more flexible and able to respond to opportunities that come your way. Open yourself so magical things can happen.

CREATIVE GENIUS
TIP #4

TUNE IN TO YOUR SENSES

Whether it's the sky, the people around you, your pets, the wind, it's time to take notice. What is happening right now around you? What can you see? What do you hear? What do you smell? Can you smell the fragrance of flowers in a vase or is it the aroma of the meal you are about to eat that fills the air? Is it the sound of cars passing by, or birds singing? What can you see outside your window?

By sending love to all of it, whether it is pleasing or annoying, you become present to what is happening in your life in this moment.

It's easy to be distracted by fun, shiny objects. These distractions keep you from noticing your feelings, experiences and creative ideas. You may not notice that your creative genius is out there leaving little bread-crumbs in hopes that you will follow along.

To find the trail to your creative genius, you have to bring your aware-ness into the present, and then pay attention.

If you react to what is going on in your environment with an open heart and acceptance you become engaged with the bigger pattern that is your life. We know from quantum physics that everything around us is made of the same energy with its own intelligence and way of communicating.

You might not be able to totally understand it, but its going on all around you. When you bring your awareness to your senses, your creative genius is activated.

Did you know that trees grow more each morning while birds are singing? It's true! They measured it!

And if you extend this awareness to your own body, you might find the same combination of things you like and things you don't like.

No matter how old you feel, how out of shape you think you are, your body is your home for this life, so why not get comfortable with it? Make it a place where you enjoy spending time.

Tune in to your body. There may be parts of your physical body that aren't doing so well. Maybe you need to move more, rethink your diet, drink more water or get more sleep. If you listen, you'll find out what you need to do to bring your beautiful body into balance.

TIP #4:

Do a candid assessment of what your health is like right now. If there are some things you want to change, this may be your opportunity to create a wellness plan. Get yourself some support for making the changes that result in vibrant health and a sense of being at home in your body.

And is there anything you need to change to feel more at home in your environment? What little things can you bring into your workplace or your home to nourish your senses?

CREATIVE GENIUS
TIP #5

WHAT GOES AROUND COMES AROUND

Before you toss your bad attitude around you like litter, take a deep breath and remember everything is a choice (because it is). And then choose to be kind to those around you.

You can be firm, you can stand up for yourself and set boundaries with others, and it is possible to do all these things without being mean.

Goodness goes a long way. I'm not saying you need to be a Pollyanna. Simply consider what other people are feeling and struggling with and see if you can help them with a smile, a cup of coffee – anything that encourages them to go on.

The time you invest in encouraging the people you care about creates a two-way energy field where your creative genius is also nourished.

While you are at it, devote some time to strengthening your ability to give and receive. If you are an independent person used to solving problems on your own, asking for help may make you feel vulnerable and weak.

My advice is that you try asking for help and see what happens. You may be pleasantly surprised!

Another secret is that if you find yourself in need of something that you are not getting, consider giving it to someone else first.

TIP #5:
Create flow by paying it forward. Look for an opportunity to do a small or big thing to help someone else. You might even up the value of what you are doing for someone else by making sure no one even knows you did it.

And while you are you are honing your understanding of the cycle of give and take, see if you can practice asking someone nicely for some help. Then open up and let yourself receive their gift.

CREATIVE GENIUS
TIP #6

FIND A WAY TO IMPROVE THE WORLD

The miracle of life is that the sun comes up and the sun goes down every day. And you and I, we have the opportunity to experience this miracle. And part of the bargain in return for being able to wake up in the morning, is that you must claim and use the gifts that have been given.

You are amazing, and there is only one of you in this great big universe we live in. And that universe wants to feel the imprint of your creative genius gifts!

Whether you choose to rescue dogs, raise kids or plant a garden, your contributions count, and they add to the legacy of human achievement.

Don't do things to be seen, or for the sake of acknowledgment. You don't need to strive for the Nobel Prize. Do them because you are here and you have your own purpose to fulfill. By expressing your creative genius, you are leaving your unique brushstroke on the world. So embrace your life, even if you spend the day doing something that no one really notices.

You are your own special brand and your secret sauce matters. So do something good to make this world a better place.

Tip #6:
Today, make your contribution. You decide what this will be – picking up trash, getting out to vote, or negotiating world peace!

Find a place to pitch in, roll up your sleeves and do your part to change the world for good with your creative genius.

CREATIVE GENIUS
TIP #1

TAP DEEPLY INTO INTO CREATIVE GENIUS

One of the most powerful ways to access your creative genius is by daydreaming.

Daydreaming is really the default modus operandi of your brain. And when you take charge of it and direct your daydreams towards a positive experience or something you can see yourself doing in the future, your body's chemistry changes.

Yes, positive daydreaming fills your body with serotonin and oxytocin, the elixirs of life.

Daydreaming rewires your brain. It opens the window for great ideas to drop in. It gives you a break to explore your awesome inner world.

Picture one thing you want to change.
Or something you wish were a part
of your life. Imagine it as if you were
watching a movie with you as the star.
Picture the thing you envision as really
happening, and do this everyday.

I guarantee you that your world will
shift before your very own eyes and
that daydream will become your reality.

TIP #7:

Right now, stop what you are doing and fantasize about your creative genius life. Just take one aspect of your world that you want to enhance or expand, and use your imagination to explore it further. Close your eyes and double click on your fantasy experience: a new job; a healthy bank balance; a loving relationship.

Let yourself imagine it with all your heart, with all the feeling you can muster. Feeling plus images equals the power to change things.

CREATIVE GENIUS
TIP #8

STOP TALKING AND LISTEN

We spend an enormous amount of time just talk, talk, talking, telling people what we think about our experiences. Unfortunately, most of us spend very little time listening, really listening to the people around us. Listening to someone is an act of love. It tells the person who is speaking 'you are important to me, you are valuable'.

Listening is action. It means you are actively engaged in the process, not just head nodding and waiting for the other person to take a breath so you can jump in with your opinion or advice.

When you listen, you hear the other person's perspective, their emotions, and their truth. The world is divided right now in many ways. We take sides over politics or civil rights or environmental issues. There is a lot of talking (and finger pointing) and not much listening. Listening helps to create a better platform for dialogue, it opens the way for understanding and the ability to find common ground.

Good listening means putting down your technological device and making eye contact, asking the person some questions and inviting them to "Tell me more..." or responding with an actual comment, "She did what!?" or "Wow, that sounds like it was really tough!"

People aren't actually looking for your advice most of the time. They just want to be heard, to be witnessed. Be a good steward of dialogue.

To understand those around you, listen first and talk later.

TIP #8:
When you are going about your day, check to see if you are truly listening. If you find yourself talking a lot, put on an inner timer. Check to see if you really have something to say, or if you need to listen.

Practice good listening skills as you move through your day. If you find yourself in the grocery store, ask the clerk about her day. And then really listen to her. She is telling you about her experience and her life. Thank her for telling you her story.

CREATIVE GENIUS TIP #9

COMMUNE WITH YOUR CREATIVE GENIUS

Spend time building a relationship with your creative genius. In ancient Rome, a genius was thought to be a genie that would follow you around and whisper insights into your ear. To enhance your ability to hear those whispers, you need to hone your ability to communicate with your creative genius.

Some people do this through stillness, others simply walk in nature mulling over an idea or issue.

Creative genius speaks in images or symbols. It might come as a flash of insight in the shower. You might hear a high-pitched sound in your ears when you need to pay attention. A message on a billboard could validate an idea. Your creative genius has its own special language for speaking to you. Your job is to develop a relationship with the source of your creative genius and get the conversation going.

Of course you can also develop your relationship with your creative genius in pure silence.

Inside of you is a whole world to be explored. When we were young we never worried about whether we were in dialogue with our inner genius genie! We followed it wherever it led us and let our imagination loose.

TIP #9
Have a conversation with your creative genius.

If you are working on a challenge or idea, get a piece of paper and write out your question. Then listen carefully for the answer. Look for images and symbols. Study the patterns of your own creative genius. What environments bring it on? Allow yourself to play with abandon and ask your creative genius to guide you. It does anyway, but your active engagement will bring surprise and delight into your day.

Ending.
(sigh)

We've come to the end, but this is just
the beginning for Creative Genius You.
Keep us posted on your progress...

email: Info@upyourcreativegenius.com
twitter: pdobrowolski
Fb: upyourcreativegenius

Special thanks to...

 Julie Boardman for love & support;

 Patricia Kryitsi Howell for editing magnificence;

 Scott Ward for his infinite creativity;

 Daz & Peyton for monitoring & unbridled love.

These pages are blank on purpose in case you wanted to draw or write something. ;-O

CPSIA information can be obtained
at www.ICGtesting.com
Printed in the USA
LVHW071922021218
599022LV00022B/984/P